How to get every Earned Value M
(EVM) Question on the PMP® Ex....
PMP Exam Prep Simplified Series of mini-e-
books
(50+ PMP® Exam Prep Sample Questions and
Solutions
on Earned Value Management)

More books by
Aileen Ellis, PgMP, PMP

PMP Exam Simplified -5th Edition
Gain knowledge and confidence to pass the PMP Exam by utilizing
over 1,000 sample questions and detailed solutions (AME Group
2013)

CAPM Exam Simplified -5th Edition
Gain knowledge and confidence to pass the CAPM Exam by
utilizing over 800 sample questions and detailed solutions (AME
Group 2013)

How to get every Contract Calculation Question right on the PMP®
Exam –
PMP Exam Prep Simplified Series of mini-e-books
(50+ PMP® Exam Prep Sample Questions and Solutions
on Contract Calculations
(AME Group 2014)

How to get every Network Diagram Question right on the PMP®
Exam – PMP Exam Prep Simplified Series of mini-e-books
(50+ PMP® Exam Prep Sample Questions and Solutions
on Network Diagrams, Crashing, Etc.)
(AME Group Coming late 2014)

How to get every Financial Question right on the PMP® Exam -
PMP Exam Prep Simplified Series of mini-e-books
(50+ PMP® Exam Prep Sample Questions and Solutions
on NPV, IRR, ROI, Etc.)
(AME Group Coming late 2014)

How to get every Statistical based Question right on the PMP®
Exam – PMP Exam Prep Simplified Series of mini-e-books
(50+ PMP® Exam Prep Sample Questions and Solutions
on standard deviation, variance, probability, Etc.)
(AME Group Coming late 2014)

To Alex, Nick and Terry
For all your patience and support
with our books and our business

Preface

In the last 16 years, I have helped over 10,000 project managers in my workshops obtain their PMP® credential. When they come into the workshop, the topic of earned value management (EVM) is typically a little scary.

After the exam, most of my students say that the exam was the hardest exam they have ever taken. When I ask them how they felt about earned value management on the exam they make comments such as:

"Earned Value Management on the exam was a no – brainer."
"Earned Value Management on the exam was so easy."

Many will even say very quietly with a smile and a wink:

"I think I got every Earned Value Management Question on the exam right.

I believe my students do so well on the EVM questions because I just love teaching EVM as well as any and all topics to do with the PMP® Exam.

For me the best way to prepare for the exam is through hundreds, if not thousands of sample questions.

I hope these questions help you so much that you walk out of the PMP® Exam with your PMP® Credential in hand and smiling and saying…

"I think I got every Earned Value Management Question right."

About the Author

Aileen Ellis, PgMP®, PMP®, is The PMP® Expert. She is the owner and proudly the only instructor for AME Group Inc., a Registered Education Provider (REP®) through the Project Management Institute (PMI®). She personally instructs project managers to gain the confidence and knowledge to pass the PMP® Exam, the CAPM® Exam and the PgMP® Exam. She has helped more than 10,000 professionals obtain their PMP® and over 1,000 professionals obtain those coveted letters: CAPM®. Working with thousands of students from dozens of countries, Ms. Ellis has gained a thorough understanding of the ins and outs of the PMBOK® Guide, the exam content, and proven test-taking strategies.

Ms. Ellis began teaching Exam Preparation Courses in 1998. Over the years she has mastered how students learn best and has incorporated those lessons and methods into her books. Her approach is focused on understanding the Project Management Processes and their interactions, with limited memorization. Ms. Ellis not only leads workshops to help students study for and pass the CAPM®, PMP®, and PgMP® exams through review of content and hundreds of sample questions, she provides materials (books, sample questions) to other REP®s and PMI® Chapters to support their educational efforts.

Set Up of the book:

Part One- Some basic ideas on Earned Value Management and a short Video Class

Part Two- 50+ Earned Value Management Questions. My suggestion is that you take notes on paper as you are working through these questions. Absolutely write down the answer you picked and why you picked that answer.

Part Three- 50+ Detailed Solutions on Earned Value Management. Make sure you review every question and that if you see questions similar to these questions on the PMP® Exam you are sure you will get every one right. Good Luck.

Part One

Some notes on Earned Value Management.
Here is a video I created on earned value management.
The video provides a basic understanding of the
earned value management system (EVM).

If you have a print copy of the book please go to my
youtube channel:
https://www.youtube.com/user/aileenellis9

BAC = Budget at completion. This is the project
budget. The BAC is usually used in relation to the
entire project. At times though BAC will be used to
represent the total budget for a single task.

PV = Planned Value. This is the plan of how much
work should be complete today. Historically, PV has
been called the BCWS. BCWS stands for budgeted cost
of work scheduled. The term BCWS should not be on
the exam.

EV = Earned Value. This is the budgeted cost of the
work completed. Historically, EV has been called the
BCWP. BCWP stands for budgeted cost of work
performed. The term BCWP should not be on the
exam.

AC = Actual cost. This is the amount of money that
has been spent for the work completed. Historically,
AC has been called the ACWP. ACWP stands for the
actual cost of work performed. The term ACWP should
not be on the exam.

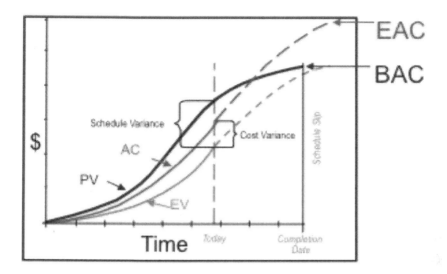

SV = Schedule variance.
SV = EV - PV.
If the project is behind schedule the SV will be a negative number.
If the project is on schedule the SV will = 0.
If the project is ahead of schedule the SV will be a positive number.
SV does not take into account critical path versus non-critical path activities.

CV = Cost variance
CV = EV – AC.
If the project is over budget the CV will be a negative number.
If the project is on budget the CV will = 0.
If the project is under budget the CV will be a positive number.

SPI = Schedule performance index.
SPI = EV/PV.
If the project is behind schedule the SPI will be less than one.
If the project is on schedule the SPI will = 1.
If the project is ahead of schedule the SPI will be greater than one.

CPI = Cost performance index.
CPI = EV/AC.
If the project is over budget the CPI will be less than one.
If the project is on budget the CPI will = 1.
If the project is under budget the CPI will be greater than one.

EAC = Estimate at completion.
There are multiple equations for EAC depending on the assumptions made.

EAC= BAC/CPI.
We use this equation if we believe the project will continue to spend at the same rate.

EAC = AC + (BAC-EV).
We use this equation if we believe that future expenditures will occur at the original forecasted amount.

EAC = AC + ((BAC-EV)/(SPI*CPI))
We use this equation if we believe that both current cost and current schedule performance will impact future cost performance.
You do not need to be able to derive this equation but let me explain it just for fun.

Actual cost (AC) is the cost of the work already complete.

(BAC-EV) represents the original estimate of the work remaining. Remember, BAC is our original budget for the entire project. Earned value (EV) is the budgeted cost of the work completed. The difference between these two numbers is the original estimate for the work remaining.

(BAC-EV) is being divided by (CPI * SPI). CPI is your cost performance index. SPI is your schedule performance index. If both the CPI and the SPI equal 1 then the division does not influence the EAC calculation.

The smaller their result (CPI*SPI) the larger the EAC will be. This makes sense. The more we are over budget and behind schedule, the larger our estimate will be for the total cost (EAC).

The greater their result (CPI*SPI) the smaller the EAC will be. This makes sense. The more we are under budget and ahead of schedule the smaller the EAC will be.

VAC = Variance at completion.
VAC= BAC - EAC.
If we forecast the project will run over budget the VAC will be a negative number.
If we forecast the project will run under budget the VAC will be a positive number.

TCPI = To complete performance index
TCPI = Budgeted cost of work remaining/ money remaining

There are multiple equations to calculate TCPI.

TCPI = (BAC-EV)/(BAC-AC).
We use this equation if we must finish the project within the BAC.

TCPI = (BAC-EV)/(EAC-AC).
We use this equation if we must finish the project within the EAC.

A TCPI that is less than one is easier to achieve.
A TCPI that is greater than one is harder to achieve.

Earned Value Measurement Methods- there are multiple methods to measure earned value. We will discuss four here.

Fixed formula- a specific percentage of the PV (planned value) is assigned to the start of a work package (or activity) and the remaining percentage is assigned to the completion. It is often used for smaller work packages.

0/100 rule. The activity obtains 0% credit when the activity begins and 100% credit when the activity is completed. The 0/100 rule is often used for material delivery.

20/80 rule. The activity obtains 20% credit when the activity begins and 80% credit when the activity is completed.

50/50 rule. The activity obtains 50% credit when the activity begins and 50% credit when the activity is completed.

Weighted milestone- this method breaks the work package into milestones. A weighted value is assigned to the completion (not partial completion) of each milestone. Often used for longer work packages with tangible outputs.

Percent complete- at the end of each time period the percent of the work package completed is multiplied by the BAC of the work package to calculate the earned value (EV). For this method to have real meaning, the measurement of percent completed should be as objective as possible.

Ex. The value (BAC) of the work package is $1000. 75% of the work is complete and therefore the EV (earned value) for the work package is 75% of $1,000= $750.

Physical measurement- relates very much to the amount of work completed.

Ex. 1,000 feet of cable should be laid on the construction project. 600 feet of cable have been laid and therefore the EV (earned value) is $600.

Part Two

1. Based on the diagram the project is currently?

a. ahead of schedule and under budget
b. ahead of schedule and over budget
c. behind schedule and under budget
d. behind schedule and over budget

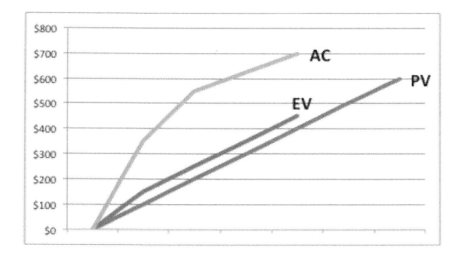

2. You are taking over the role of project manager on a project to build a training facility for horses. Earned value management (EVM) is being used on the project and you have been handed some incomplete information. For your project, the cost performance index (CPI) = 1.2. The actual cost (AC) = $75,000. The planned value (PV) = $60,000. What is the earned value (EV) for this project?

a. $50,000
b. $62,500
c. $72,000
d. $90,000

3. For your project the earned value (EV) = $500. The actual cost (AC) = $100. The planned value (PV) = $300. What is the schedule variance (SV)?

a. $200
b. $100
c. -$100
d. -$200

4. In the earned value management (EVM) system what term represents the budgeted cost of the work scheduled to be completed as of today?

a. planned value (PV)
b. earned value (EV)
c. actual cost (AC)
d. budget at completion (BAC)

5. For the project the earned value (EV) = $500. The actual cost (AC) = $300. The planned value (PV) = $400. The project is:

a. ahead of schedule and under budget
b. behind schedule and under budget
c. ahead of schedule and over budget
d. behind schedule and over budget

6. For the project the earned value (EV) = $350. The actual cost (AC) = $280. The planned value (PV) = $500. The total project budget is $1,000. Assume that you will continue to spend at the same rate as you are currently spending. What is the project's estimate at completion (EAC)?

a. $800
b. $930
c. $1,000
d. $1,023

7. Work package 1.5.2.3 on your project has a budget at completion (BAC) of $4,000. Since this work package is small and is planned to be complete within two reporting periods it was decided to use the 50/50 fixed formula method for reporting earned value. Work package 1.5.2.3 has just started and very little work is complete on it. You must report on earned value today. At this point you would report an earned value of:

a. $0
b. $1
c. $2,000
d. $4,000

8. A schedule performance index (SPI) of .82 means:

a. 82% of the work planned to be complete as of today is completed
b. 82% of the total project work is completed
c. 82% of the project budget has been spent
d. 82% of the budget planned to be spent as of today is spent

9. The estimate at completion (EAC) for the project is $140,000. The cost performance index (CPI) is .80. What is the project's budget at completion (BAC)?

a. $112,000
b. $140,000
c. $175,000
d. $220,000

10. For your project the earned value (EV) = $250. The actual cost (AC) = $200. The planned value (PV) = $400. What is the schedule performance index (SPI)?

a. 1.25
b. 0.80
c. 0.625
d. 1.60

11. The schedule performance index (SPI) is .75 and the cost performance index (CPI) is .80. The project is:

a. ahead of schedule and under budget
b. behind schedule and under budget
c. ahead of schedule and over budget
d. behind schedule and over budget

12. For your project the earned value (EV) = $350. The actual cost (AC) = $280. The planned value (PV) = $500. The total project budget is $1,000. Assume the remaining work will be influenced by both current cost and current schedule performance. What is the project's estimate at completion (EAC)?

a. $800
b. $930
c. $1,023
d. $1,480

13. For the project the earned value (EV) = $350. The actual cost (AC) = $400. The planned value (PV) = $500. The total project budget is $1,000. Assume that you will continue to spend at the same rate as you are currently spending. What is the project's variance at completion (VAC)?

a. -$143
b. +$143
c. -$125
d. +$125

14. For the project the earned value (EV) = $350. The actual cost (AC) = $280. The planned value (PV) = $500. The total project budget is $1,000. Assume the original estimate was flawed. Your engineering team has given you a new estimate for the remaining work of $1,200. What is the project's estimate to complete (ETC)?

a. $800
b. $930
c. $1,200
d. $1,480

15. Work package 1.2.2.3 on your project has a total budget of $5,000. Since this work package is small and is planned to be complete within two reporting periods it was decided to use the 50/50 fixed formula method for reporting earned value. Work package 1.2.2.3 is 98 % complete as of today. At this point you should report an earned value of:

a. $0
b. $2,500
c. $4,900
d. $5,000

16. For your project the earned value (EV) = $250. The actual cost (AC) = $200. The planned value (PV) = $400. What is the cost performance index (CPI)?

a. 1.25
b. 0.80
c. .625
d. 1.60

17. You are taking over the role of project manager on a project to bring refrigeration systems to independent farmers with no reliable power. Earned value management (EVM) is being used on the project. The previous project manager provided you incomplete information. For the project the cost performance index (CPI) = 0.8. The earned value (EV) = $120,000. The planned value (PV) = $60,000. What is the actual cost (AC) for this project?

a. $48,000
b. $75,000
c. $96,000
d. $150,000

18. Based on the following table what is the schedule variance (SV) for the project?

	Planned Value (PV)	Total Value (BAC)	Actual Cost (AC)	% Complete of Total
Activity K	$3,000	$3,000	$3,500	100%
Activity L	$2,400	$3,000	$2,700	60%
Activity M	$1,400	$3,000	$1,700	50%

a. -$500
b. -$1,000
c. -$1,600
d. -$2,700

19. In the earned value system what term represents the budgeted cost of the work completed as of today?

a. planned value (PV)
b. earned value (EV)
c. actual cost (AC)
d. budget at completion (BAC)

20. The project is to rebuild a historic bridge as part of a long-term community restoration project. The total budget is $500,000. Time is moving fast. We are at the end of month nine of a twelve-month project. 90% of the total work is complete. $360,000 has been spent for the work that is complete. The cost performance index (CPI) is:

a. 1.25
b. 1.20
c. .90
d. .80

21. Based on the diagram the project is currently?

a. ahead of schedule and under budget
b. ahead of schedule and over budget
c. behind schedule and under budget
d. behind schedule and over budget

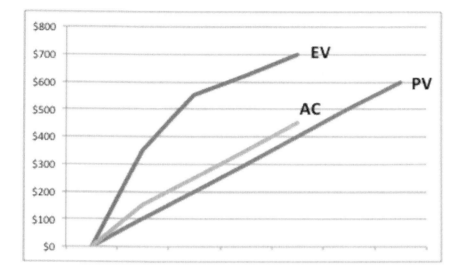

22. Work package 1.3.2.8 on your project has a budget at completion (BAC) of $20,000. Since the work package relates to the receipt of materials it was decided to use the 0/100 fixed formula method for reporting earned value. Work package 1.3.2.8 is running late and is near completion though not actually completed. You must report earned value on this work package today at your monthly review. You should report an earned value of:

a. $0
b. $1
c. $19,500
d. $20,000

23. For your project the earned value (EV) = $280. The actual cost (AC) = $350. The planned value (PV) = $260. The total project budget is $500. Assume that you will continue to spend at the same rate as you are currently spending. What is the project's estimate at completion (EAC)?

a. $625
b. $570
c. $609
d. $500

24. For your project the earned value (EV) = $280. The actual cost (AC) = $350. The planned value (PV) = $260. The total project budget is $500. Assume the current variances are atypical and that the remaining work will be completed using original estimates. What is the project's estimate at completion (EAC)?

a. $625
b. $570
c. $609
d. $500

25. Your project is running over budget and behind schedule. Which of the following would be true regarding the cost performance index (CPI) and the schedule performance index (SPI)?

a. CPI > 1 and SPI > 1
b. CPI > 1 and SPI < 1
c. CPI < 1 and SPI > 1
d. CPI < 1 and SPI < 1

26. Based on the following table what is the earned value (EV) for the project?

	Planned Value (PV)	Total Value (BAC)	Actual Cost (AC)	% Complete of Total
Activity A	$3,000	$3,000	$2,500	100%
Activity B	$2,400	$3,000	$2,700	80%
Activity C	$400	$3,000	$800	50%

a. $5,800
b. $6,000
c. $6,900
d. $9,000

27. Work package 1.2.2.8 on your project has a budget at completion (BAC) of $10,000. Since the work package relates to the receipt of materials it was decided to use the 0/100 fixed formula method for reporting earned value. Work package 1.2.2.8 actually completed ahead of schedule. You must report earned value on this work package today at your monthly review. You should report an earned value of:

a. $0
b. $1
c. $9,500
d. $10,000

28. A schedule performance index (SPI) of 1.30 means:

a. the activities are 30% ahead of schedule based on the critical path method
b. the project is running 30% over budget
c. the project is progressing at 130% of the rate expected, looking at all activities
d. the project is running 30% under budget

29. For your project the earned value (EV) = $280. The actual cost (AC) = $350. The planned value (PV) = $260. The total project budget is $500. Assume that you will continue to spend at the same rate as you are currently spending. What is the to-complete-performance-index (TCPI) required to finish the work within the forecasted estimate at completion (EAC)?

a. 0.80
b. 0.90
c. 1.11
d. 1.25

30. You are managing a minor system upgrade for your organization's website. The budget is $1,400. As of today you should have $700 worth of work completed. You have only $350 worth of work completed and you have spent $200 to complete this work.
What is the cost variance (CV) for the project?

a. +$150
b. +$350
c. +$500
d. -$350

31. The schedule performance index (SPI) is .75 and the cost performance index (CPI) is 1.25. The project is:

a. ahead of schedule and under budget
b. behind schedule and under budget
c. ahead of schedule and over budget
d. behind schedule and over budget

32. You are taking over the role of project manager on a project to bring clean water to people who live in very dry communities. Earned value management (EVM) is being used on the project. The previous project manager provided you incomplete information. For your project the schedule performance index (SPI) = 0.8. The earned value (EV) = $120,000. The actual cost (AC) = $60,000. What is the planned value (PV) for this project?

a. $ 48,000
b. $ 75,000
c. $ 96,000
d. $150,000

33. In the earned value system what term represents the actual cost of the work accomplished?

a. planned value (PV)
b. earned value (EV)
c. actual cost (AC)
d. budget at completion (BAC)

34. For your project the earned value (EV) = $350. The actual cost (AC) = $280. The planned value (PV) = $500. The total project budget is $1,000. Assume the original estimate was flawed. Your engineering team has given you a new estimate for the remaining work of $1,200. What is the project's estimate at completion (EAC)?

a. $800
b. $930
c. $1,023
d. $1,480

35. Work package 1.7.2 is one of your larger work packages. In fact the work on this package is expected to cross several reporting periods. Milestones have been set up and it has been decided to use the weighted milestone method to calculate earned value (EV). Best practices are in place allowing for one interim milestone per reporting period and no partial credit.

Here is the status as of today.

Milestone	PV	Percent Complete	EV
Milestone A	$3,000	100%	
Milestone B	$4,000	50%	
Milestone C	$5,000	0	

At this point we should report an earned value of:
a. $0
b. $3,000
c. $5,000
d. $12,000

36. For your project the earned value (EV) = $350. The actual cost (AC) = $280. The planned value (PV) = $500. The total project budget is $1,000. Assume the current variances are atypical and that the remaining work will be completed using original estimates. What is the project's estimate at completion (EAC)?

a. $800
b. $930
c. $1,023
d. $1,480

37. For your project the earned value (EV) = $350. The actual cost (AC) = $280. The planned value (PV) = $500. The total project budget is $1,000. Assume that you will continue to spend at the same rate as you are currently spending. What is the project's estimate to complete (ETC)?

a. $520
b. $800
c. $1,023
d. $1,800

38. For your project the earned value (EV) = $350. The actual cost (AC) = $280. The planned value (PV) = $500. The total project budget is $1,000. What is the to-complete-performance-index (TCPI) required to finish the work within the budget at completion (BAC)?

a. 0.80
b. 0.90
c. 1.11
d. 1.25

39. Based on the following table what is the cost performance index (CPI) for the project?

	Planned Value (PV)	Total Value (BAC)	Actual Cost (AC)	% Complete of Total
Activity D	$2,500	$2,500	$2,500	100%
Activity E	$2,500	$2,500	$2,700	80%
Activity F	$1,250	$2,500	$1,500	50%

a. 1.16
b. .86
c. .92
d. 1.09

40. The project is to rebuild a historic bridge as part of a long-term community restoration project. The total budget is $500,000. Time is moving fast. We are at the end of month nine of a twelve-month schedule. The budget is constant for each month. 90% of the total work is completed. $360,000 has been spent for the work that is complete. The schedule performance index (SPI) is:

a. 1.25
b. 1.20
c. .90
d. .80

41. Based on the diagram the project is currently?

a. ahead of schedule and under budget
b. ahead of schedule and over budget
c. behind schedule and under budget
d. behind schedule and over budget

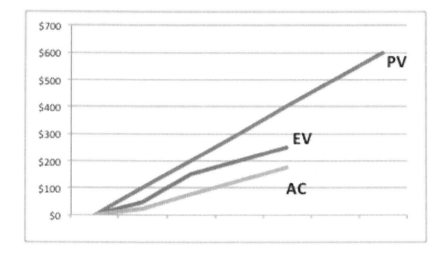

42. A cost performance index (CPI) of .80 means:

a. the project is progressing at 80% of the rate planned
b. the project is running 80% over budget
c. 80% of the budget planned to be spent as of today has been spent
d. for every dollar we spend on the project we are getting 80 cents of value

43. Work package 1.3.2 is one of your larger work packages. In fact the work on this package is expected to cross several reporting periods. Therefore, milestones have been set up and it has been decided to use the weighted milestone method to calculate earned value. Best practices are in place allowing for one interim milestone per reporting period and no partial credit.
Here is the status as of today.

Weighted Milestones	1st	2nd	3rd
Planned Value	$5,000	$5,000	$5,000
Percent Complete	100%	100%	25%

At this point we should report an earned value of:
a. $0
b. $5,000
c. $10,000
d. $11,250

44. Based on the table below what is the schedule performance index (SPI) for the project?

	Planned Value (PV)	Total Value (BAC)	Actual Cost (AC)	% Complete of Total
Activity D	$2,500	$2,500	$2,500	100%
Activity E	$2,500	$2,500	$2,700	80%
Activity F	$1,250	$2,500	$1,500	50%

a. 1.16
b. .86
c. .92
d. .09

45. Your project is running under budget and ahead of schedule. Which of the following would be true regarding the cost performance index (CPI) and the schedule performance index (SPI)?

a. CPI > 1 and SPI >1
b. CPI > 1 and SPI <1
c. CPI < 1 and SPI >1
d. CPI < 1 and SPI <1

46. You are taking over the role of project manager on a project to raise funds for cancer research. Earned value management is being used on the project and you have been handed some incomplete information. For your project the cost variance (CV) = $40,000 and the actual cost (AC) = $20,000. What is the earned value (EV) for this project?

a. -$20,000
b. +$20,000
c. +$40,000
d. +$60,000

47. For your project the earned value (EV) = $280. The actual cost (AC) = $350. The planned value (PV) = $260. The total project budget is $500. Assume that you will continue to spend at the same rate as you are currently spending. What is the project's variance at completion (VAC)?

a. -$625
b. -$570
c. -$275
d. -$125

48. For your project the earned value (EV) = $500.
The actual cost (AC) = $300. The planned value (PV) =
$400. What is cost variance (CV)?

a. $ 200
b. $ 400
c. $ 500
d. -$ 200

49. The project is scheduled to last for six months. The budget for each month is $200 and expected to stay constant for the life of the project. You have just completed month four of the project. Thirty (30) percent of the total work is complete and you have spent sixty (60) percent of the total budget. The schedule variance (SV) for this project is:

a. -$440
b. -$360
c. +$440
d. +$360

50. Work package 1.4.3 is planned to take 1,000 hours of labor to complete. The cost of the labor is $45/hour. Due to the nature of the work package it was decided to use the percent complete method for calculating earned value. At this point 500 hours have been spent on the work package and 30% of the work is complete. The earned value (EV) we should report is:

a. $0
b. $13,500
c. $22,500
d. $45,000

Bonus Question #1-

I believe this question is too tricky for the exam. I have included it here just in case.

Your project is to rebuild a historic bridge as part of a long-term community restoration project. The total budget is $500,000. Time seems to be moving fast. The project is half way through the schedule. Only 30% of the work that was scheduled to be complete as of today is complete today. $280,000 has been spent for the work that is complete. The earned value (EV) for this project is:

a. $500,000
b. $280,000
c. $150,000
d. $ 75,000

Bonus Question #2.

The project has a total budget of $150,000. The planned value is $75,000. As of today one third of the work is complete. Fifty percent of the "budget to date" has been spent. What is the actual cost (AC)?
a. $0
b. $37,500
c. $75,000
d. $150,000

Bonus Question #3.

The project is to transfer technology developed in your factory in Rio to an operations facility in China. There are approximately 2,000 stakeholders on the project living in 7 different countries. Your sponsor is very involved and communicates regularly with you, the project management team, and the key stakeholders. Your CPI is .95 and the project is running 14 weeks behind schedule. Based on this scenario what should you be most concerned about?

a. schedule
b. cost
c. stakeholder management
d. sponsor management

Bonus Question 4.
This bonus question comes from:

How to get every Network Diagram Question right on the PMP®
Exam right – PMP Exam Prep Simplified Series of mini-e-books
(50+ PMP® Exam Prep Sample Questions and Solutions
on Network Diagrams, Crashing, Etc.)
(AME Group Coming late 2014)

The project schedule shows a duration of 47 weeks. After careful review management has decided that the project must finish within 42 weeks. They ask you and your team to develop a plan to crash the schedule based on cost. There are five activities on the critical path that can be crashed. Activity A has a duration of 8 weeks and can be shortened by 2 weeks for a cost of $4,000. Activity F has a duration of 9 weeks and can be shortened by 4 weeks for a cost of $16,000. Activity J has a duration of 12 weeks and can be shortened by 1 week for a cost of $2,000. Activity K has a duration of 5 weeks and can be shortened by 2 weeks for a cost of $2,000. Activity R has a duration of 8 weeks and can be shortened by 3 weeks for a cost of $9,000.
The activities that should be crashed are:

a. Activity A and Activity R
b. Activity K and Activity R
c. Activity A and Activity J and Activity K
d. Activity F and Activity J

Bonus Question 5.
This bonus question comes from:

How to get every Financial Question right on the PMP® Exam –
PMP Exam Prep Simplified Series of mini-e-books
(50+ PMP® Exam Prep Sample Questions and Solutions
on NPV, IRR, ROI, Etc.)
(AME Group Coming late 2014)

The portfolio review board is conducting a project selection review. They are going to make their decision based on the Net Present Value (NPV) estimates for the projects. The organization has only $100,000 available for investment. Based on the following information which project should they select? Assume an interest rate of 5%.

Project A - The initial investment = $100,000. The benefit at end of year one = $40,000. The additional benefit at end of year two = $70,000. There are no other benefits.

Project B – The initial investment = $100,000. There is no benefit at the end of year one. The benefit = $42,000 at end of year two. There is an additional benefit = $70,000 at end of year 3.

Which project(s) should they select?

a. Project A
b. Project B
c. Both projects since they each have a positive net present value.
d. Neither project since they each have a negative net present value.

Bonus Question 6.
This bonus question comes from:

How to get every Statistical based Question right on the PMP®
Exam – PMP Exam Prep Simplified Series of mini-e-books
(50+ PMP® Exam Prep Sample Questions and Solutions
on standard deviation, variance, probability, Etc.)
(AME Group Coming late 2014)

You are the project manager for a logging company.
This month you are charted to deliver 10,000 units
that are 60 centimeters each. Your upper control limit
on your process is 63 centimeters. Your lower control
limit on your process is 57 centimeters.
Approximately what percentage of your units will be
above 61 centimeters?

a. 68.3%
b. 31.7%
c. 95.5%
d. 15.9%

This bonus question comes from:

How to get every Contract Calculation Question right on the
PMP® Exam – PMP Exam Prep Simplified Series of mini-e-
books
(50+ PMP® Exam Prep Sample Questions and Solutions
on Contract Calculations.)
(AME Group 2014)

A Fixed Price Incentive Fee (FPIF) contract has the
following parameters:
Target Cost = $200,000
Target Profit = $20,000
Target Price = $220,000
Ceiling Price = $250,000
Share Ratio 70/30

The project was completed for an actual cost of
$170,000. What is the actual profit the seller receives?

a. $9,000
b. $11,000
c. $20,000
d. $29,000

Part Three

1. **Based on the diagram the project is currently?**

a. ahead of schedule and under budget
b. ahead of schedule and over budget
c. behind schedule and under budget
d. behind schedule and over budget

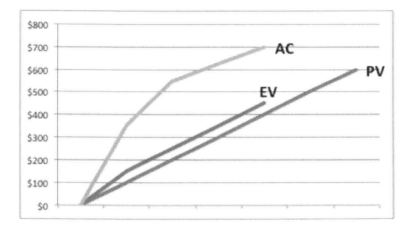

Solution:
Answer (b) is the best answer.
Always begin with the earned value (EV) to solve problems that ask about ahead or behind schedule and under or over budget.

Since the earned value (EV) > planned value (PV) the project is running ahead of schedule. We have more work completed (EV) than scheduled (PV).

Since the earned value (EV) < actual cost (AC) the project is running over budget. We have less work completed (EV) than money spent (AC).

2. You are taking over the role of project manager on a project to build a training facility for horses. Earned value management (EVM) is being used on the project and you have been handed some incomplete information. For your project, the cost performance index (CPI) = 1.2. The actual cost (AC) = $75,000. The planned value (PV) = $60,000. What is the earned value (EV) for this project?

a. $50,000
b. $62,500
c. $72,000
d. $90,000

Solution:
Answer (d) is the best answer.
This is an equation manipulation question. If you look at your equation list you probably do not have an equation to calculate earned value (EV).
In this question we are given the cost performance index (CPI), the actual cost (AC), and the planned value (PV). We are asked to calculate earned value (EV). Do you have an equation with three of these terms including earned value (EV)? Most likely you have the equation:

CPI= EV/AC.
We want to solve for EV. Therefore, we want to get EV alone on one side of the equal sign. Multiply both sides of the equation by AC.
AC * CPI = AC * (EV/AC). The two ACs will eliminate each other on the right side of the equation.
AC * CPI = EV.
$75,000 (1.2) = EV
$90,000 = EV
Note that we did not use PV. On the exam, we may be given data that we do not need to solve the problem. I call this distractor information.

© AME Group Inc. August 2014

3. **For your project the earned value (EV) = $500. The actual cost (AC) = $100. The planned value (PV) = $300. What is the schedule variance (SV)?**

a. $200
b. $100
c. -$100
d. -$200

Solution:
Answer (a) is the best answer.
Schedule Variance (SV)= earned value (EV) - planned value (PV)
SV = EV - PV
SV = $500 – $300 = $200.

EV > PV. The budgeted cost of the work completed (EV) is greater than the budgeted value of the work scheduled (PV). The project is ahead of schedule. NOTE- we did not need to use AC to answer this question.
In the diagram the EV line (the budgeted cost of how much work is complete) is higher than the PV (the budgeted cost of work scheduled to be completed today) line. Therefore, I know the answer will be a positive number.

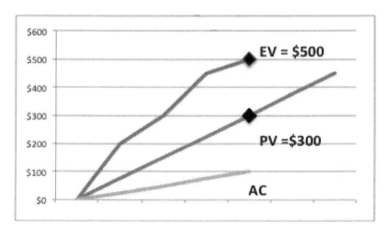

4. In the earned value management (EVM) system what term represents the budgeted cost of the work scheduled to be completed as of today?

a. planned value (PV)
b. earned value (EV)
c. actual cost (AC)
d. budget at completion (BAC)

Solution:
Answer (a) is the best answer.

PV	Planned Value	How much work was scheduled to be complete as of today?
EV	Earned Value	How much work was completed as of today?
AC	Actual Cost	How much did we spend for the work completed?
BAC	Budget at Completion	What is the total budget for the project?
EAC	Estimate at Completion	Based on what we know now how much do we expect the who project to cost?
ETC	Estimate to Complete	How much more do we need to spend over what we have already spent?
VAC	Variance at Completion	How much do we expect to vary from the BAC?

5. For the project the earned value (EV) = $500. The actual cost (AC) = $300. The planned value (PV) = $400. The project is:

a. ahead of schedule and under budget
b. behind schedule and under budget
c. ahead of schedule and over budget
d. behind schedule and over budget

Solution:
Answer (a) is the best answer.

Schedule performance index (SPI) = EV/PV
SPI = $500/$400= 1.25.
1.25 >1. A SPI >1 is good. The project is ahead of schedule.

Cost performance index (CPI) = EV/AC
CPI = $500/$300 = 1.67
1.67 > 1. A CPI > 1 is good. The project is under budget.

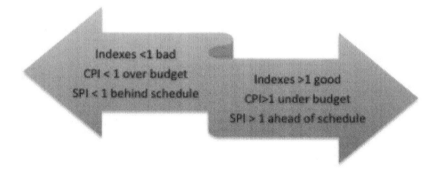

6. For the project the earned value (EV) = $350. The actual cost (AC) = $280. The planned value (PV) = $500. The total project budget is $1,000. Assume that you will continue to spend at the same rate as you are currently spending. What is the project's estimate at completion (EAC)?

a. $800
b. $930
c. $1,000
d. $1,023

Solution:
Answer (a) is the best answer.

There are multiple equations for Estimate at Completion (EAC).

Use the equation: EAC = BAC/CPI for the assumption: We will continue to spend at the same rate.

Use the equation: EAC = AC + (BAC - EV) for the assumption: Current variances are seen as atypical and the remaining work will be completed using original estimates.

Use the equation: EAC = AC + ((BAC-EV)/(SPI*CPI)) for the assumption: The remaining work will be influenced by both current schedule and current cost performance.

Use the equation: EAC = AC + bottom-up ETC for the assumption: The initial plan is no longer valid.

Choose the equation that matches the assumption that we will continue to spend at the same rate.

EAC= BAC/CPI.

BAC stands for budget at completion, which is the total project budget. In this example the BAC is given as $1,000.

CPI stands for cost performance index.

CPI= EV/AC.

CPI= $350/$280 = 1.25.

EAC = BAC/CPI = 1,000/1.25 = $800.

Since the EAC < BAC we forecast to under run the project.

7. **Work package 1.5.2.3 on your project has a budget at completion (BAC) of $4,000. Since this work package is small and is planned to be complete within two reporting periods it was decided to use the 50/50 fixed formula method for reporting earned value. Work package 1.5.2.3 has just started and very little work is complete on it. You must report on earned value today. At this point you would report an earned value of:**

a. $0
b. $1
c. $2,000
d. $4,000

Solution:
Answer (c) is the best answer.
The question states that the 50/50 fixed formula method will be used for reporting earned value. With this method a work package gets 50% earned value credit when it starts and the other 50% earned value credit when it is completed. In this example the work package has started and has not completed.
Therefore, 50% earned value credit can be taken. 50% of a BAC of $4,000= $2,000.
The earned value we can report is $2,000.

The table contrasts the 0/100, the 50/50, and the 25/75 methods.

Method	Start	Finish	Total BAC
0/100	0% $0	100% $4,000	$4,000
50/50	50% $2,000	50% $2,000	$4,000
25/75	25% $1,000	75% $3,000	$4,000

8. A schedule performance index (SPI) of .82 means:

a. 82% of the work planned to be complete as of today is completed
b. 82% of the total project work is completed
c. 82% of the project budget has been spent
d. 82% of the budget planned to be spent as of today is spent

Solution:
Answer (a) is the best answer.
SPI = EV/PV
A SPI of .82 means the project is progressing at 82% of the rate expected. We do not know how much work is completed (EV) by just looking at SPI. We only know how much work is completed (EV) as compared to how much was planned to be completed (PV) as of today. The SPI tells us nothing about how much of the project budget has been spent (AC).

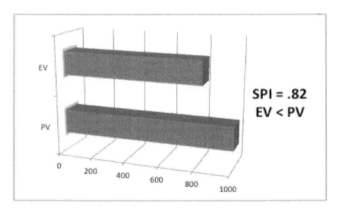

9. The estimate at completion (EAC) for the project is $140,000. The cost performance index (CPI) is .80. What is the project's budget at completion (BAC)?

a. $112,000
b. $140,000
c. $175,000
d. $220,000

Solution:
Answer (a) is the best answer.

This is an equation manipulation question. We know the EAC and the CPI and we want to calculate BAC. To solve we need to look for an equation that contains EAC, CPI, and BAC. If no assumption is given in the question we should assume that we will continue to spend at the same rate. The equation we will use is:

EAC= BAC/CPI.
To solve for BAC we multiply both sides of the equation by CPI.

(CPI) * (EAC) = (CPI) * (BAC/CPI).
The two CPIs will cancel each other out on the right side of the equation.

(CPI)* (EAC) = BAC.
(0.8)*($140,000) = BAC
BAC= $112,000

Note- This problem could be solved without doing any math.
Since the CPI is less than one, I know I am over running the project budget. Therefore, the project budget (the BAC) must be less than the EAC of $140,000. Answer (a) is the only answer less than the EAC of $140,000.

10. **For your project the earned value (EV) = $250. The actual cost (AC) = $200. The planned value (PV) = $400. What is the schedule performance index (SPI)?**

a. 1.25
b. 0.80
c. 0.625
d. 1.60

Solution:
Answer (c) is the best answer.

Schedule performance index (SPI) = EV/PV
SPI = $250/$400= .625.
.625 < 1. A SPI < 1 is bad. The project is behind schedule.

11. The schedule performance index (SPI) is .75 and the cost performance index (CPI) is .80. The project is:

a. ahead of schedule and under budget
b. behind schedule and under budget
c. ahead of schedule and over budget
d. behind schedule and over budget

Solution:
Answer (d) is the best answer.
SPI = .75.
.75 < 1. Indexes < 1 are bad. The project is behind schedule.
SPI = EV/PV. If SPI < 1 then the EV < PV.
This means we have less work completed (EV) than work scheduled (PV).
We are behind schedule.

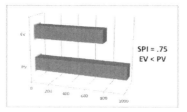

CPI = .80.
.80 < 1. Indexes < 1 are bad. The project is over budget.
CPI = EV/AC. If CPI < 1 than the EV < AC.
This means we have less work completed (EV) than money spent (AC) for that work. We are over budget.

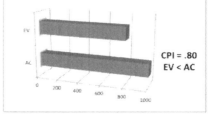

12. **For your project the earned value (EV) = $350. The actual cost (AC) = $280. The planned value (PV) = $500. The total project budget is $1,000. Assume the remaining work will be influenced by both current cost and current schedule performance. What is the project's estimate at completion (EAC)?**

a. $800
b. $930
c. $1,023
d. $1,480

Solution:
Answer (c) is the best answer.

There are multiple equations for Estimate at Completion (EAC).

Use the equation: EAC = BAC/CPI for the assumption: We will continue to spend at the same rate.

Use the equation: EAC = AC + (BAC - EV) for the assumption: Current variances are seen as atypical and the remaining work will be completed using original estimates.

Use the equation: EAC = AC + ((BAC-EV)/(SPI*CPI)) for the assumption: The remaining work will be influenced by both current schedule and current cost performance.

Use the equation: EAC = AC + bottom-up ETC for the assumption: The initial plan is no longer valid.

Choose the equation that matches the assumption that the remaining work will be influenced by both current cost and schedule performance.

EAC = AC + (BAC-EV)/(CPI*SPI).

AC = $280. This was a given.
BAC - EV= $1,000 - $350 = $650

CPI= EV/AC= $350/$280 = 1.25
SPI = EV/PV = $350/ $500 = .70
CPI * SPI= 1.25 * .70 = .875

EAC = AC + (BAC-EV)/(CPI*SPI)
EAC = $280 + ($650/.875)
EAC= $280 + $743
EAC= $1,023

13. For the project the earned value (EV) = $350. The actual cost (AC) = $400. The planned value (PV) = $500. The total project budget is $1,000. Assume that you will continue to spend at the same rate as you are currently spending. What is the project's variance at completion (VAC)?

a. -$143
b. +$143
c. -$125
d. +$125

Solution:
Answer (a) is the best answer.

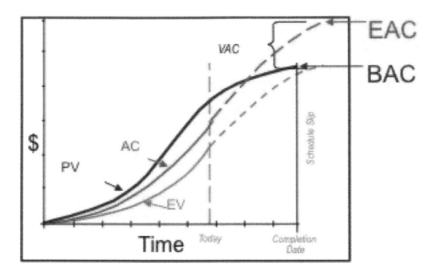

VAC = BAC- EAC
BAC stands for budget at completion, which is the total project budget. In this example the BAC is given as $1,000.
EAC= BAC/CPI.
CPI stands for cost performance index.
CPI= EV/AC.
CPI= $350/$400= .875
EAC = BAC/CPI = $1,000/.875 = $1,143.

VAC= BAC- EAC
VAC= $1,000- $1,143
VAC= -$143
Since this answer is a negative number we are forecasting that we will over run the project budget (BAC).

14. For the project the earned value (EV) = $350. The actual cost (AC) = $280. The planned value (PV) = $500. The total project budget is $1,000. Assume the original estimate was flawed. Your engineering team has given you a new estimate for the remaining work of $1,200. What is the project's estimate to complete (ETC)?

a. $800
b. $930
c. $1,200
d. $1,480

Solution:
Answer (c) is the best answer.

Estimate to complete (ETC) is a forecast of how much we need to spend over what we have already spent for the project.
In some ways this is a trick question.
The question gives us the answer.

The engineering team's estimate for the remaining work of $1,200 is their forecast of how much more we need to spend to complete the project (ETC).

15. **Work package 1.2.2.3 on your project has a total budget of $5,000. Since this work package is small and is planned to be complete within two reporting periods it was decided to use the 50/50 fixed formula method for reporting earned value. Work package 1.2.2.3 is 98 % complete as of today. At this point you should report an earned value of:**

a. $0
b. $2,500
c. $4,900
d. $5,000

Solution:
Answer (b) is the best answer.
The question states that the 50/50 fixed formula method will be used for reporting earned value. With this method a work package gets 50% earned value credit for starting and the other 50% earned value credit when it is completed. In this example, the work package has started and has not completed.
Therefore, 50% earned value credit can be taken. 50% of a BAC of $5,000 = $2,500.
With the 50/50 fixed formula method it does not matter when calculating earned value if the work package is 2% complete or 98% complete. All that matters is if the work package has started and if it has finished.

The table contrasts the 0/100, the 50/50, and the 25/75 methods.

Method	Start	Finish	Total BAC
0/100	0% $0	100% $5,000	$5,000
50/50	50% $2,500	50% $2,500	$5,000
25/75	25% $1,250	75% $3,750	$5,000

© AME Group Inc. August 2014

16. For your project the earned value (EV) = $250. The actual cost (AC) = $200. The planned value (PV) = $400. What is the cost performance index (CPI)?

a. 1.25
b. 0.80
c. .625
d. 1.60

Solution:
Answer (a) is the best answer.

Cost performance index (CPI) = EV/AC
CPI = $250/$200 = 1.25
1.25 > 1. A CPI > 1 is good. The project is under budget.

17. **You are taking over the role of project manager on a project to bring refrigeration systems to independent farmers with no reliable power. Earned value management (EVM) is being used on the project. The previous project manager provided you incomplete information. For the project the cost performance index (CPI) = 0.8. The earned value (EV) = $120,000. The planned value (PV) = $60,000. What is the actual cost (AC) for this project?**

a. $48,000
b. $75,000
c. $96,000
d. $150,000

Solution:
Answer (d) is the best answer.
This is an equation manipulation question. If you look at your equation list you probably do not have an equation to calculate actual cost (AC).
In this question we are given the cost performance index (CPI), the earned value (EV), the planned value (PV), and asked to calculate the actual cost (AC). Do you have an equation with three of these terms including actual cost (AC)? Most likely you have the equation:

$CPI = EV/AC$.
We want to solve for AC. Therefore, we want AC alone on one side of the equal sign preferably in the numerator.
Multiply both sides of this equation by AC.
$AC * CPI = AC * (EV/AC)$. The two ACs on the right side will cancel each other out.

$AC * CPI = EV$. Now divide both sides by CPI.
$(AC * CPI) / CPI = EV/ CPI$. The two CPIs on the left side will cancel each other out.
$AC = EV/CPI$. Now solve.

© AME Group Inc. August 2014

AC = $120,000/0.8

AC = $150,000. Since the CPI is less than one it makes sense that the actual cost (AC) would be greater than the budgeted cost of the work complete (EV).

Note that we did not use PV in our calculation. On the exam we may be given data that we do not need to solve the problem. I call this distractor information.

18. Based on the following table what is the schedule variance (SV) for the project?

	Planned Value (PV)	Total Value (BAC)	Actual Cost (AC)	% Complete of Total
Activity K	$3,000	$3,000	$3,500	100%
Activity L	$2,400	$3,000	$2,700	60%
Activity M	$1,400	$3,000	$1,700	50%

a. -$500
b. -$1,000
c. -$1,600
d. -$2,700

Solution:
Answer (a) is the best answer.
SV= EV - PV.
Earned value (EV) is the budgeted cost of the work completed.
On the exam use the percent complete method unless the question tells you differently.
The BAC of Activity K is $3,000. It is 100% complete.
The earned value of Activity K is $3,000.
The BAC of Activity L is $3,000. It is 60% complete.
The earned value of Activity L is 60% of $3,000 = $1,800.
The BAC of Activity M is $3,000. It is 50% complete.
The earned value of Activity M is 50% of $3,000 = $1,500.
The earned value for the project =
$3,000+$1,800+$1,500 = $6,300

Planned value (PV) is the budgeted cost of the work scheduled to be complete as of today.

The table tells us the planned value (PV) for the project.
PV = $3,000+$2,400+$1,400.
PV= $6,800. This is the budgeted cost of how much work should be complete as of today.

SV= EV-PV
SV = $6,300 - $6,800 = -$500. The answer is negative because the project is behind schedule.

	Planned Value (PV)	Total Value (BAC)	Actual Cost (AC)	% Complete of Total	Earned Value
Activity K	$3,000	$3,000	$3,500	100%	$3,000
Activity L	$2,400	$3,000	$2,700	60%	$1,800
Activity M	$1,400	$3,000	$1,700	50%	$1,500
Project Total	$6,800	$9,000	$7,900		$6,300

19. In the earned value system what term represents the budgeted cost of the work completed as of today?

a. planned value (PV)
b. earned value (EV)
c. actual cost (AC)
d. budget at completion (BAC)

Solution:
Answer (b) is the best answer.

PV	Planned Value	How much work was scheduled to be complete as of today?
EV	Earned Value	How much work was completed as of today?
AC	Actual Cost	How much did we spend for the work completed?
BAC	Budget at Completion	What is the total budget for the project?
EAC	Estimate at Completion	Based on what we know now how much do we expect the who project to cost?
ETC	Estimate to Complete	How much more do we need to spend over what we have already spent?
VAC	Variance at Completion	How much do we expect to vary from the BAC?

20. The project is to rebuild a historic bridge as part of a long-term community restoration project. The total budget is $500,000. Time is moving fast. We are at the end of month nine of a twelve-month project. 90% of the total work is complete. $360,000 has been spent for the work that is complete. The cost performance index (CPI) is:

a. 1.25
b. 1.20
c. .90
d. .80

Solution:
Answer (a) is the best answer.

$CPI = EV/AC$.

Earned value (EV) is the budgeted cost of the work completed.
90% of the total work is complete. The budgeted cost of the total work is $500,000.
$EV = 90\% * \$500,000$
$EV = \$450,000$

$AC = \$360,000$

$CPI = EV/AC$
$CPI = \$450,000/\$360,000$
$CPI = 1.25$

21. Based on the diagram the project is currently?

a. ahead of schedule and under budget
b. ahead of schedule and over budget
c. behind schedule and under budget
d. behind schedule and over budget

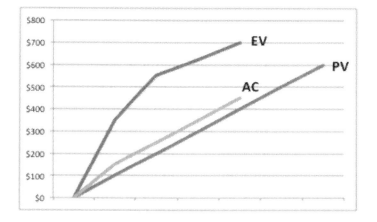

Solution:
Answer (a) is the best answer.
Always begin with the earned value (EV) to solve problems that ask about ahead or behind schedule and under or over budget.

Since the earned value (EV) > planned value (PV) the project is running ahead of schedule. We have more work complete (EV) than scheduled (PV).

Since the earned value (EV) > actual cost (AC) the project is running under budget. We have more work complete (EV) than money spent (AC).

22. **Work package 1.3.2.8 on your project has a budget at completion (BAC) of $20,000. Since the work package relates to the receipt of materials it was decided to use the 0/100 fixed formula method for reporting earned value. Work package 1.3.2.8 is running late and is near completion though not actually completed. You must report earned value on this work package today at your monthly review. You should report an earned value of:**

a. $0
b. $1
c. $19,500
d. $20,000

Solution:
Answer (a) is the best answer.
The question states that we are using the 0/100 fixed formula method to calculate earned value. With the 0/100 fixed formula method a work package receives 0% earned value credit when it starts and 100% earned value credit when it is completed. The question states that the work package is near completion. Near completion is still not complete. Therefore, this work package received $0 earned value credit at this point.

The table contrasts the 0/100, the 50/50, and the 25/75 methods.

Method	Start	Finish	Total BAC
0/100	0% $0	100% $20,000	$20,000
50/50	50% $10,000	50% $10,000	$20,000
25/75	25% $5,000	75% $15,000	$20,000

23. **For your project the earned value (EV) = $280. The actual cost (AC) = $350. The planned value (PV)**

= $260. The total project budget is $500. Assume that you will continue to spend at the same rate as you are currently spending.   What is the project's estimate at completion (EAC)?

a. $625
b. $570
c. $609
d. $500

Solution:
Answer (a) is the best answer.

There are multiple equations for Estimate at Completion (EAC).

Use the equation: EAC = BAC/CPI for the assumption: We will continue to spend at the same rate.

Use the equation: EAC = AC + (BAC - EV) for the assumption: Current variances are seen as atypical and the remaining work will be completed using original estimates.

Use the equation: EAC = AC + ((BAC-EV)/(SPI*CPI)) for the assumption: The remaining work will be influenced by both current schedule and current cost performance.

Use the equation: EAC = AC + bottom-up ETC for the assumption: The initial plan is no longer valid.

Choose the equation that matches the assumption that we will continue to spend at the same rate.

EAC= BAC/CPI.
Budget at completion (BAC) is the total project budget. In this example the BAC is given as $500.

CPI stands for cost performance index. The equation is: CPI= EV/AC.

CPI= \$280/\$350 = .80

EAC = BAC/CPI = \$500/.80 = \$625.

Since the EAC > BAC we are forecasting the project will run over budget.

24. For your project the earned value (EV) = $280. The actual cost (AC) = $350. The planned value (PV) = $260. The total project budget is $500. Assume the current variances are atypical and that the remaining work will be completed using original estimates. What is the project's estimate at completion (EAC)?

a. $625
b. $570
c. $609
d. $500

Solution:
Answer (b) is the best answer.
There are multiple equations for Estimate at Completion (EAC).

Use the equation: EAC = BAC/CPI for the assumption: We will continue to spend at the same rate.
Use the equation: EAC = AC + (BAC - EV) for the assumption: Current variances are seen as atypical and the remaining work will be completed using original estimates.
Use the equation: EAC = AC + ((BAC-EV)/(SPI*CPI)) for the assumption: The remaining work will be influenced by both current schedule and current cost performance.
Use the equation: EAC = AC + bottom-up ETC for the assumption: The initial plan is no longer valid.
Choose the equation that matches the assumption that the current variances are atypical and that the remaining work will be completed using original estimates.

EAC = AC + (BAC-EV).
EAC= AC + (BAC - EV) = $350 + ($500 - $280) = $350 + $220 = $570.

25. Your project is running over budget and behind schedule. Which of the following would be true

regarding the cost performance index (CPI) and the schedule performance index (SPI)?

a. CPI > 1 and SPI > 1
b. CPI > 1 and SPI < 1
c. CPI < 1 and SPI > 1
d. CPI < 1 and SPI < 1

Solution:
Answer (d) is the best answer.

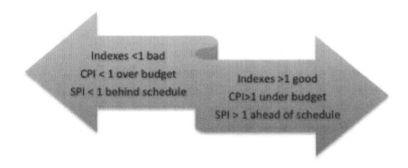

26. Based on the following table what is the earned value (EV) for the project?

	Planned Value (PV)	Total Value (BAC)	Actual Cost (AC)	% Complete of Total
Activity A	$3,000	$3,000	$2,500	100%
Activity B	$2,400	$3,000	$2,700	80%
Activity C	$400	$3,000	$800	50%

a. $5,800
b. $6,000
c. $6,900
d. $9,000

Solution:
Answer (c) is the best answer.
Earned Value (EV) is the budgeted cost of the work completed.
On the exam use the percent complete method unless the question tells you differently.
The BAC of Activity A is $3,000. It is 100% complete.
The earned value of Activity A is $3,000.
The BAC of Activity B is $3,000. It is 80% complete.
The earned value of Activity B is 80% of $3,000 = $2,400.
The BAC of Activity C is $3,000. It is 50% complete.
The earned value of Activity C is 50% of $3,000 = $1,500.

The total earned value (EV) for the project is = $3,000 + $2,400 + $1,500.
EV = $6,900.

	Planned Value (PV)	Total Value (BAC)	Actual Cost (AC)	% Complete of Total	Earned Value
Activity A	$3,000	$3,000	$2,500	100%	$3,000
Activity B	$2,400	$3,000	$2,700	80%	$2,400
Activity C	$400	$3,000	$800	50%	$1,500
Project Total	$5,800	$9,000	$6,000		$6,900

© AME Group Inc. August 2014

27. Work package 1.2.2.8 on your project has a budget at completion (BAC) of $10,000. Since the work package relates to the receipt of materials it was decided to use the 0/100 fixed formula method for reporting earned value. Work package 1.2.2.8 actually completed ahead of schedule. You must report earned value on this work package today at your monthly review. You should report an earned value of:

a. $0
b. $1
c. $9,500
d. $10,000

Solution:
Answer (d) is the best answer.
The question states that we are using the 0/100 fixed formula method to calculate earned value. With the 0/100 fixed formula method a work package receives 0% earned value credit for starting and 100% earned value credit for completing. The question states that the work package is complete. Regardless of if the work package completes early, on time, or late, it still receives 100% earned value credit when complete. Therefore, the earned value we should report is the full BAC of $10,000.

Method	Start	Finish	Total BAC
0/100	0%	100%	
	$0	$10,000	$10,000
50/50	50%	50%	
	$5,000	$5,000	$10,000
25/75	25%	75%	
	$2,500	$7,500	$10,000

28. A schedule performance index (SPI) of 1.30 means:

a. the activities are 30% ahead of schedule based on the critical path method
b. the project is running 30% over budget
c. the project is progressing at 130% of the rate expected, looking at all activities
d. the project is running 30% under budget

Solution:
Answer (c) is the best answer.

SPI= EV/PV

An SPI of 1.30 means the project is progressing at 130% of the rate expected. We do not know how much work is complete by just looking at SPI. SPI does not take into account critical path versus non-critical path activities. We only know how much work is complete (EV) as compared to how much was planned to be complete (PV) as of today. The SPI tells us nothing about how much of the project budget has been spent.

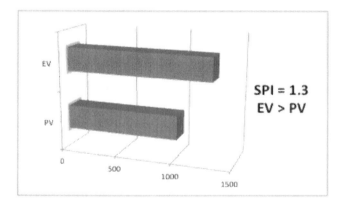

© AME Group Inc. August 2014

29. For your project the earned value (EV) = $280. The actual cost (AC) = $350. The planned value (PV) = $260. The total project budget is $500. Assume that you will continue to spend at the same rate as you are currently spending. What is the to-complete-performance-index (TCPI) required to finish the work within the forecasted estimate at completion (EAC)?

a. 0.80
b. 0.90
c. 1.11
d. 1.25

Solution:
Answer (a) is the best answer.

Assumption	Equation for To Complete Performance Index (TCPI)
TCPI	TCPI = (budgeted cost of work remaining/money remaining)
The project must be completed on plan. (The project must be completed within the BAC)	TCPI = (BAC-EV)/(BAC-AC)
The project must be completed within the current EAC.	TCPI= (BAC-EV)/(EAC-AC)

The question asks what is the TCPI required to finish within the forecasted EAC.
TCPI = (budgeted cost of work remaining/money remaining).
Work remaining = (BAC-EV).
Money remaining in this example = (EAC-AC). EAC is in this equation and not BAC because the question states we must finish within our forecasted EAC.

Since the question tells us to assume we will continue to spend at the same rate as current spending we can use the equation: EAC= BAC/CPI.

Budget at completion (BAC) is the total project budget. In this question the BAC is given as $500.
CPI stands for cost performance index. The equation is: CPI= EV/AC.
CPI= $280/$350 = .80
EAC = BAC/CPI = $500/.80 = $625.

Now back to TCPI.
TCPI= (BAC-EV)/(EAC-AC).
TCPI = ($500 - $280)/($625 - $350).
TCPI = ($220)/($275)
TPCI = .8
The means the project needs to continue to spend at the same rate (as the CPI) to finish within the EAC.

30. You are managing a minor system upgrade for your organization's website. The budget is $1,400. As of today you should have $700 worth of work completed. You have only $350 worth of work completed and you have spent $200 to complete this work.

What is the cost variance (CV) for the project?

a. +$150
b. +$350
c. +$500
d. -$350

Solution:
Answer (a) is the best answer.

Cost variance (CV) = earned value (EV) - actual cost (AC).
Earned value (EV) is the budgeted cost of the work completed.
$350 worth of work is complete.
EV = $350.

Actual cost (AC) is the amount of money you have spent for the work completed.
AC = $200

Cost variance (CV) = (EV) - (AC)
CV = $350 - $200 = $150
The cost variance (CV) is a positive number.
We have more work complete (EV) than actual money spent (AC).
The planned value (PV) of $700 is not required to solve the problem.

31. The schedule performance index (SPI) is .75 and the cost performance index (CPI) is 1.25. The project is:

a. ahead of schedule and under budget
b. behind schedule and under budget
c. ahead of schedule and over budget
d. behind schedule and over budget

Solution:
Answer (b) is the best answer.
SPI = .75
 .75 < 1. Indexes < 1 are bad. The project is behind schedule.
SPI = EV/PV. If SPI < 1 then the EV < PV.
We have less work complete (EV) than work scheduled (PV). We are behind schedule.

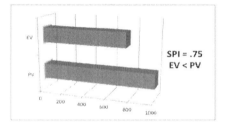

CPI = 1.25. 1.25 > 1. Indexes > 1 are good. The project is under budget.
CPI= EV/AC. If CPI > 1 than EV > AC.
We have more work complete (EV) than money spent (AC) for that work. We are under budget.

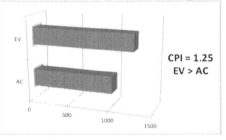

32. **You are taking over the role of project manager on a project to bring clean water to people who live in very dry communities. Earned value management (EVM) is being used on the project. The previous project manager provided you incomplete information. For your project the schedule performance index (SPI) = 0.8. The earned value (EV) = $120,000. The actual cost (AC) = $60,000. What is the planned value (PV) for this project?**

a. $ 48,000
b. $ 75,000
c. $ 96,000
d. $150,000

Solution:
Answer (d) is the best answer.
This is an equation manipulation question. If you look at your equation list you probably do not have an equation to calculate planned value (PV).
In this question we are given the schedule performance index (SPI), the earned value (EV), the actual cost (AC), and asked to calculate the planned value (PV). Do you have an equation with three of these terms including planned value (PV)? Most likely you have the equation:

$SPI = EV/PV$.
We want to solve for PV. Therefore, we want PV alone on one side of the equal sign preferably in the numerator.
Multiply both sides of this equation by PV.
$PV * SPI = PV * (EV/PV)$. The two PVs on the right side will cancel each other out.

$PV * SPI = EV$. Now divide both sides by SPI.
$(PV * SPI) / SPI = EV/ SPI$. The two SPIs on the left side will cancel each other out.
$PV = EV /SPI$.
$PV = \$120,000/.8$

PV = $150,000. Since the SPI is less than one it makes sense that the budgeted cost of the work scheduled (PV) would be larger than the budgeted cost of the work completed (EV).

Note that we did not use AC in our calculation. On the exam we may be given data that we do not need to solve the problem. I call this distractor information.

33. In the earned value system what term represents the actual cost of the work accomplished?

a. planned value (PV)
b. earned value (EV)
c. actual cost (AC)
d. budget at completion (BAC)

Solution:
Answer (c) is the best answer.

PV	Planned Value	How much work was scheduled to be complete as of today?
EV	Earned Value	How much work was completed as of today?
AC	Actual Cost	How much did we spend for the work completed?
BAC	Budget at Completion	What is the total budget for the project?
EAC	Estimate at Completion	Based on what we know now how much do we expect the who project to cost?
ETC	Estimate to Complete	How much more do we need to spend over what we have already spent?
VAC	Variance at Completion	How much do we expect to vary from the BAC?

34. For your project the earned value (EV) = $350. The actual cost (AC) = $280. The planned value (PV) = $500. The total project budget is $1,000. Assume the original estimate was flawed. Your engineering team has given you a new estimate for the remaining work of $1,200. What is the project's estimate at completion (EAC)?

a. $800
b. $930
c. $1,023
d. $1,480

Solution:
Answer (d) is the best answer.

There are multiple equations for Estimate at Completion (EAC).

Use the equation: EAC = BAC/CPI for the assumption: We will continue to spend at the same rate.
Use the equation: EAC = AC + (BAC - EV) for the assumption: Current variances are seen as atypical and the remaining work will be completed using original estimates.
Use the equation: EAC = AC + ((BAC-EV)/(SPI*CPI)) for the assumption: The remaining work will be influenced by both current schedule and current cost performance.
Use the equation: EAC = AC + bottom-up ETC for the assumption: The initial plan is no longer valid.

Choose the equation that matches the assumption that the original estimate was flawed.
EAC = AC + bottom-up ETC
EAC= $280 + $1,200
EAC= $1,480

35. Work package 1.7.2 is one of your larger work packages. In fact the work on this package is expected to cross several reporting periods.

Milestones have been set up and it has been decided to use the weighted milestone method to calculate earned value (EV). Best practices are in place allowing for one interim milestone per reporting period and no partial credit.
Here is the status as of today.

Milestone	PV	Percent Complete	EV
Milestone A	$3,000	100%	
Milestone B	$4,000	50%	
Milestone C	$5,000	0	

At this point we should report an earned value of:
a. $0
b. $3,000
c. $5,000
d. $12,000

Solution:
Answer (b) is the best answer.
The question states that we are using the weighted milestone method to calculate earned value and we are following the best practice of no partial credit for milestones. Therefore:

Milestone	PV	Percent Complete	EV
Milestone A	$3,000	100%	$3,000
Milestone B	$4,000	50%	$0
Milestone C	$5,000	0	$0

36. For your project the earned value (EV) = $350. The actual cost (AC) = $280. The planned value (PV) = $500. The total project budget is $1,000. Assume the current variances are atypical and that the remaining work will be completed using original estimates. What is the project's estimate at completion (EAC)?

a. $800
b. $930
c. $1,023
d. $1,480

Solution:
Answer (b) is the best answer.

There are multiple equations for Estimate at Completion (EAC).

Use the equation: EAC = BAC/CPI for the assumption: We will continue to spend at the same rate.

Use the equation: EAC = AC + (BAC - EV) for the assumption: Current variances are seen as atypical and the remaining work will be completed using original estimates.

Use the equation: EAC = AC + ((BAC-EV)/(SPI*CPI)) for the assumption: The remaining work will be influenced by both current schedule and current cost performance.

Use the equation: EAC = AC + bottom-up ETC for the assumption: The initial plan is no longer valid.

Choose the equation that matches the assumption that the current variances are atypical and that the remaining work will be completed using original estimates.

EAC = AC + (BAC-EV).

EAC = $280 + ($1,000 – $350)

EAC = $280 + $650

EAC = $930

37. For your project the earned value (EV) = $350. The actual cost (AC) = $280. The planned value (PV) = $500. The total project budget is $1,000. Assume that you will continue to spend at the same rate as you are currently spending. What is the project's estimate to complete (ETC)?

a. $520
b. $800
c. $1,023
d. $1,800

Solution:
Answer (a) is the best answer.

ETC= EAC – AC

EAC= BAC/CPI since we are assuming we will continue to spend at the same rate.

BAC stands for budget at completion, which is the total project budget. In this question the BAC is given as $1,000.
CPI stands for cost performance index.
CPI= EV/AC.
CPI= $350/$280 = 1.25.
EAC = BAC/CPI = $1,000/1.25 = $800.

ETC = EAC- AC
ETC= $800-$280
ETC= $520

38. For your project the earned value (EV) = $350. The actual cost (AC) = $280. The planned value (PV) = $500. The total project budget is $1,000. What is the to-complete-performance-index (TCPI) required to finish the work within the budget at completion (BAC)?

a. 0.80
b. 0.90
c. 1.11
d. 1.25

Solution-
Answer (b) is the best answer.

Assumption	Equation for To Complete Performance Index (TCPI)
TCPI	TCPI= (budgeted cost of work remaining/money remaining)
The project must be completed on plan. (The project must be completed within the BAC)	TCPI = (BAC-EV)/(BAC-AC)
The project must be completed within the current EAC.	TCPI= (BAC-EV)/(EAC-AC)

The question asks what is the TCPI required to finish within the BAC.

TCPI= (BAC-EV)/(BAC-AC).
TCPI = ($1,000 - $350)/($1000 - $280).
TCPI = ($650)/($720)
TPCI = ~.903

39. Based on the following table what is the cost performance index (CPI) for the project?

	Planned Value (PV)	Total Value (BAC)	Actual Cost (AC)	% Complete of Total
Activity D	$2,500	$2,500	$2,500	100%
Activity E	$2,500	$2,500	$2,700	80%
Activity F	$1,250	$2,500	$1,500	50%

a. 1.16
b.   .86
c.   .92
d. 1.09

Solution:
Answer (b) is the best answer.

Cost performance index (CPI) = EV/AC

Earned value (EV) is the budgeted cost of the work completed.
On the exam use the percent complete method unless the question tells you differently.
The BAC of Activity D is $2,500. It is 100% complete.
The earned value of Activity D is $2,500.
The BAC of Activity E is $2,500. It is 80% complete.
The earned value of Activity E is 80% of $2,500 = $2,000.
The BAC of Activity F is $2,500. It is 50% complete.
The earned value of Activity F is 50% of $2,500 = $1,250.
The earned value for the project = $2,500+$2,000+$1,250 = $5,750.

The actual cost (AC) is the actual amount of money spent to date for the work completed. The AC = $2,500 +$2,700 + $1,500 = $6,700.

CPI= EV/AC = $5,750 / $6,700 = .86. Since the CPI is less than 1 the project is running over budget.

	Planned Value (PV)	Total Value (BAC)	Actual Cost (AC)	% Complete of Total	Earned Value
Activity D	$2,500	$2,500	$2,500	100%	$2,500
Activity E	$2,500	$2,500	$2,700	80%	$2,000
Activity F	$1,250	$2,500	$1,500	50%	$1,250
Project Total	$6,250	$7,500	$6,700		$5,750

40. The project is to rebuild a historic bridge as part of a long-term community restoration project. The total budget is $500,000. Time is moving fast. We are at the end of month nine of a twelve-month schedule. The budget is constant for each month. 90% of the total work is completed. $360,000 has been spent for the work that is complete. The schedule performance index (SPI) is:

a. 1.25
b. 1.20
c. .90
d. .80

Solution:
Answer (b) is the best answer.

SPI= EV/PV.

EV is the budgeted cost of the work that is completed. 90% of the total work is complete. The budgeted cost of the total work is $500,000.
EV = 90% * $500,000
EV = $450,000

PV is the budgeted cost of the work that was scheduled to be complete as of today. The question states the project is at the end of month nine of a twelve month schedule. Since the budget is constant for each month
PV = (9months/12months) * $500,000.
PV = $375,000

SPI = EV/PV
SPI= $450,000/$375,000
SPI = 1.2

41. Based on the diagram the project is currently?

a. ahead of schedule and under budget
b. ahead of schedule and over budget
c. behind schedule and under budget
d. behind schedule and over budget

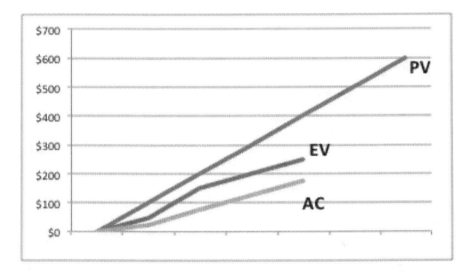

Solution:
Answer (c) is the best answer.

Always begin with the earned value (EV) to solve problems that ask about ahead or behind schedule and under or over budget.

Since the earned value (EV) < planned value (PV) the project is running behind schedule. We have less work complete (EV) than scheduled (PV).

Since the earned value (EV) > actual cost (AC) the project is running under budget. We have more work complete (EV) than money spent (AC).

42. A cost performance index (CPI) of .80 means:

a. the project is progressing at 80% of the rate planned
b. the project is running 80% over budget
c. 80% of the budget planned to be spent as of today has been spent
d. for every dollar we spend on the project we are getting 80 cents of value

Solution:
Answer (d) is the best answer.
CPI= EV/AC

CPI relates to cost and not to schedule.
A CPI of .8 means the budgeted cost of the work complete (EV) is 80% of the actual cost (AC). A CPI < 1 is bad from a cost standpoint. The CPI tells us nothing about the schedule.

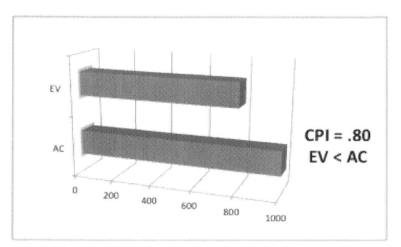

43. Work package 1.3.2 is one of your larger work packages. In fact the work on this package is expected to cross several reporting periods. Therefore, milestones have been set up and it has been decided to use the weighted milestone method to calculate earned value. Best practices are in place allowing for one interim milestone per reporting period and no partial credit.
Here is the status as of today.

Weighted Milestones	1st	2nd	3rd
Planned Value	$5,000	$5,000	$5,000
Percent Complete	100%	100%	25%

At this point we should report an earned value of:
a. $0
b. $5,000
c. $10,000
d. $11,250

Solution:
Answer (c) is the best answer.
The question states that we are using the weighted milestone method to calculate earned value and we are following the best practice of no partial credit for milestones. Therefore:

Weighted Milestones	1st	2nd	3rd
Planned Value	$5,000	$5,000	$5,000
Percent Complete	100%	100%	25%
Earned Value	$5,000	$5,000	$0

44. Based on the table below what is the schedule performance index (SPI) for the project?

	Planned Value (PV)	Total Value (BAC)	Actual Cost (AC)	% Complete of Total
Activity D	$2,500	$2,500	$2,500	100%
Activity E	$2,500	$2,500	$2,700	80%
Activity F	$1,250	$2,500	$1,500	50%

a. 1.16
b. .86
c. .92
d. .09

Solution:
The best answer is answer (c).
Schedule performance index (SPI) = EV/PV

Earned value (EV) is the budgeted cost of the work completed.
On the exam use the percent complete method unless the question tells you differently.
The BAC of Activity D is $2,500. It is 100% complete.
The earned value of Activity D is $2,500.
The BAC of Activity E is $2,500. It is 80% complete.
The earned value of Activity E is 80% of $2,500 = $2,000.
The BAC of Activity F is $2,500. It is 50% complete.
The earned value of Activity F is 50% of $2,500 = $1,250.
The earned value for the project =
$2,500+$2,000+$1,250 = $5,750.

Planned value (PV). It is the budgeted cost of the work scheduled to be complete as of today.
The question tells us the PV of the three activities.
PV for the project = $2,500 + $2,500+ $1,250
PV = $6,250

SPI= EV/PV = $5,750/$6,250 = .92
Since the SPI is less than one the project is behind
schedule according to the earned value system.

	Planned Value (PV)	Total Value (BAC)	Actual Cost (AC)	% Complete of Total	Earned Value
Activity D	$2,500	$2,500	$2,500	100%	$2,500
Activity E	$2,500	$2,500	$2,700	80%	$2,000
Activity F	$1,250	$2,500	$1,500	50%	$1,250
Project Total	$6,250	$7,500	$6,700		$5,750

45. Your project is running under budget and ahead of schedule. Which of the following would be true regarding the cost performance index (CPI) and the schedule performance index (SPI)?

a. CPI > 1 and SPI >1
b. CPI > 1 and SPI <1
c. CPI < 1 and SPI >1
d. CPI < 1 and SPI <1

Solution:
Answer (a) is the best answer.

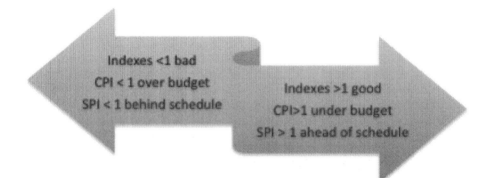

Indexes <1 bad
CPI < 1 over budget
SPI < 1 behind schedule

Indexes >1 good
CPI>1 under budget
SPI > 1 ahead of schedule

46. You are taking over the role of project manager on a project to raise funds for cancer research. Earned value management is being used on the project and you have been handed some incomplete information. For your project the cost variance (CV) = $40,000 and the actual cost (AC) = $20,000. What is the earned value (EV) for this project?

a. -$20,000
b. +$20,000
c. +$40,000
d. +$60,000

Solution:
Answer (d) is the best answer.
This is an equation manipulation question. If you look at your equation list you probably do not have an equation to calculate earned value (EV).
In this question we are given the actual cost (AC) and the cost variance (CV) and asked to calculate the earned value (EV). Do you have an equation with these three terms? Most likely you have the equation:
CV= EV-AC.
We want to solve for EV. Therefore, we want EV alone on one side of the equal sign.
We therefore add AC to both sides to get EV alone.
AC + CV = AC + EV - AC
AC + CV = EV.
$20,000 + $40,000 = EV.
$60,000 = EV.

47. **For your project the earned value (EV) = $280. The actual cost (AC) = $350. The planned value (PV) = $260. The total project budget is $500. Assume that you will continue to spend at the same rate as you are currently spending. What is the project's variance at completion (VAC)?**

a. -$625
b. -$570
c. -$275
d. -$125

Solution:
Answer (d) is the best answer.

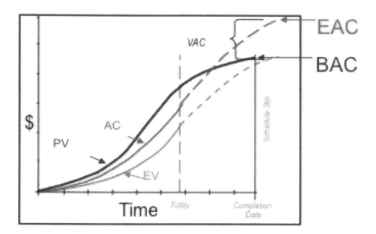

VAC= BAC- EAC

BAC stands for budget at completion, which is the total project budget. In this example the BAC is given as $500.
EAC= BAC/CPI.
CPI stands for cost performance index.
CPI= EV/AC.
CPI= $280/$350 = .80
EAC = BAC/CPI = $500/.80 = $625.

VAC = BAC- EAC

VAC = $500 - $625
VAC = - $125
Since the VAC is a negative number we are forecasting the project will overrun.

48. For your project the earned value (EV) = $500. The actual cost (AC) = $300. The planned value (PV) = $400. What is cost variance (CV)?

a. $ 200
b. $ 400
c. $ 500
d. -$ 200

Solution:
Answer (a) is the best answer.
Cost variance (CV) = earned value (EV) – actual cost (AC)
CV = EV - AC
CV = $500 -$300 = $200.
Note- we did not need to use PV to answer this question.

49. The project is scheduled to last for six months. The budget for each month is $200 and expected to stay constant for the life of the project. You have just completed month four of the project. Thirty (30) percent of the total work is complete and you have spent sixty (60) percent of the total budget. The schedule variance (SV) for this project is:

a. -$440
b. -$360
c. +$440
d. +$360

Solution:
Answer (a) is the best answer.

Schedule variance (SV) = earned value (EV) - planned value (PV).

Earned value (EV) is the budgeted cost of the work completed. The question states that 30% of the total work is complete. What is the budgeted cost of the total work? Since the project is scheduled for six months with a constant budget of $200/month the total budget is 6 months * $200/month = $1,200 total budget.
Back to earned value (EV). We have 30% of the total work complete. Earned value is 30% of $1,200= $360.
Planned value (PV) is the budgeted cost of the work scheduled to be complete as of today. The question states that we are at the end of month four. Therefore, we should have four months of work complete.
PV= 4 months * $200/month = $800.

Schedule variance (SV) = EV - PV = $360 - $800 = -$440. The answer is negative because the project is behind schedule.

50. Work package 1.4.3 is planned to take 1,000 hours of labor to complete. The cost of the labor is

$45/hour. Due to the nature of the work package it was decided to use the percent complete method for calculating earned value. At this point 500 hours have been spent on the work package and 30% of the work is complete. The earned value (EV) we should report is:

a. $0
b. $13,500
c. $22,500
d. $45,000

Solution:
Answer (b) is the best answer.

The question states that 30% of the work is complete. Since we are using the percent complete method we know that the earned value (EV) is 30% of the total work (BAC).
The total work (BAC) is 1,000 hours at $45/hour.
BAC = 1,000 * $45 = $45,000
EV = 30% of $45,000
EV = $13,500

Bonus Question #1-

I believe this question is too tricky for the exam. I have included it here just in case.

Your project is to rebuild a historic bridge as part of a long-term community restoration project. The total budget is $500,000. Time seems to be moving fast. The project is half way through the schedule. Only 30% of the work that was scheduled to be complete as of today is complete today. $280,000 has been spent for the work that is complete. The earned value (EV) for this project is:

a. $500,000
b. $280,000
c. $150,000
d. $ 75,000

Solution:
Answer (d) is the best answer. This is a tricky question. Most people taking the exam would get this question wrong.

Earned value (EV) is the budgeted cost of the work completed.
The question states that 30% of the work that should be complete as of today is complete. The real question is: How much work should be complete as of today?
The total budget (BAC) is $500,000. This represents all the project work.
The project is half way through the schedule.
Therefore, half the total work should be complete.
Planned value (PV) is the budgeted cost of the work scheduled to be complete as of today.
PV = 50% of $500,000.
PV= $250,000.
There should be $250,000 worth of work complete as of today.

30% of that work is complete (EV).
Earned value (EV) = 30% * $250,000
EV = $75,000.
NOTE- The earned value (EV) is not equal to 30% of the total budget of $500,000. If this were true the question would state that 30% of the total work is complete. The question states that 30% of the work that should be complete as of today is complete. This means that 30% of the planned value (PV) is complete. PV is the budgeted cost of the work scheduled to be complete as of today.

Bonus Question #2.

The project has a total budget of $150,000. The planned value is $75,000. As of today one third of the work is complete. Fifty percent of the "budget to date" has been spent. What is the actual cost (AC)?
a. $0
b. $37,500
c. $75,000
d. $150,000

Solution:
Answer (b) is the best answer. This question may be too tricky for the exam.

BAC= $150,000
PV = $75,000. The planned value (PV) represents how much work should be complete as of today.
EV = (1/3) * $150,000 = $50,000. The earned value (EV) represents the budgeted cost of the work complete.
AC = 50% of the "budget to date".
AC = 50% * PV
AC = 50% * $75,000
AC = $37,500.

The hard part of the question is the phrase "budget to date". The "budget to date" is the budget for the work that should be complete as of today. This is a different name for the planned value (PV).

Bonus Question #3.

The project is to transfer technology developed in your factory in Rio to an operations facility in China. There are approximately 2,000 stakeholders on the project living in 7 different countries. Your sponsor is very involved and communicates regularly with you, the project management team, and the key stakeholders. Your CPI is .95 and the project is running 14 weeks behind schedule. Based on this scenario what should you be most concerned about?

a. schedule
b. cost
c. stakeholder management
d. sponsor management

Solution:
Answer (b) is the best answer.

A CPI=.95 is a quantitative idea. This is where we
 should put our focus.
The question states that the CPI= .95 and the project is 14 weeks behind schedule. Both items sound bad. How do we decide? We look for the quantitative answer. The project is 14 weeks behind schedule. I am saying this is qualitative, not quantitative because we do not know how long the schedule is. What if the schedule is 15 years? 14 weeks may not be that bad. While we have many stakeholders there is nothing in the question to state that we have an issue that needs to be resolved.
The question states that the sponsor is communicating. Everything looks good with the Sponsor.

Bonus Question 4.
This bonus question comes from:

How to get every Network Diagram Question right on the PMP®
Exam – PMP Exam Prep Simplified Series of mini-e-books
(50+ PMP® Exam Prep Sample Questions and Solutions
on Network Diagrams, Crashing, Etc.)
(AME Group Coming late 2014)

The project schedule shows a duration of 47 weeks. After careful review management has decided that the project must finish within 42 weeks. They ask you and your team to develop a plan to crash the schedule based on cost. There are five activities on the critical path that can be crashed. Activity A has a duration of 8 weeks and can be shortened by 2 weeks for a cost of $4,000. Activity F has a duration of 9 weeks and can be shortened by 4 weeks for a cost of $16,000. Activity J has a duration of 12 weeks and can be shortened by 1 week for a cost of $2,000. Activity K has a duration of 5 weeks and can be shortened by 2 weeks for a cost of $2,000. Activity R has a duration of 8 weeks and can be shortened by 3 weeks for a cost of $9,000. The activities that should be crashed are:

a. Activity A and Activity R
b. Activity K and Activity R
c. Activity A and Activity J and Activity K
d. Activity F and Activity J

Solution:

Answer (c) is the best answer. There is a lot of data in this question. When crashing we want to save the most amount of time for the least amount of money. For the PMP Exam I most likely would create a table like the one below to help me easily solve this problem. Once I have the table I know I need to save five weeks for the least amount of money. Answer (a) will save me 5 weeks for $13,000. Answer (b) will save me 5 weeks for $11,000. Answer (c) will save me 5 weeks for $8,000. Answer (d) will save me 5 weeks for $18,000. Answer (c) is the best answer.

	Current Duration	Weeks to be saved by crashing	Cost of crashing	Cost/week of crashing
Activity A	8 weeks	2 weeks	$4,000	$2,000
Activity F	9 weeks	4 weeks	$16,000	$4,000
Activity J	12 weeks	1 week	$2,000	$2,000
Activity K	5 weeks	2 weeks	$2,000	$1,000
Activity R	8 weeks	3 weeks	$9,000	$3,000

Bonus Question 5.
This bonus question comes from:

How to get every Financial Question right on the PMP® Exam –
PMP Exam Prep Simplified Series of mini-e-books
(50+ PMP® Exam Prep Sample Questions and Solutions
on NPV, IRR, ROI, Etc.)
(AME Group Coming late 2014)

The portfolio review board is conducting a project selection review. They are going to make their decision based on the Net Present Value (NPV) estimates for the projects. The organization has only $100,000 available for investment. Based on the following information which project should they select?
Assume an interest rate of 5%.
Project A - The initial investment = $100,000. The benefit at end of year one = $40,000. The additional benefit at end of year two = $70,000. There are no other benefits.
Project B – The initial investment = $100,000. There is no benefit at the end of year one. The benefit = $42,000 at end of year two. There is an additional benefit = $70,000 at end of year 3.
Which project(s) should they select?

a. Project A
b. Project B
c. Both projects since they each have a positive net present value.
d. Neither project since they each have a negative net present value.

Solution
Answer (a) is the best answer.
Project A has a higher NPV than Project B. The NPV of
    Project A is a positive number. This means our
    estimates show we forecast to make money on
    this project.

Project A
The Present Value of $40,000 received at the end of year 1:
$PV = FV/(1+i)^t$
$PV = \$40,000/(1.05)^1$
$PV = \$38,095.23$
The Present Value of $70,000 received at the end of year 2:
$PV = FV/(1+i)^t$
$PV = \$70,000/(1.05)^2$
$PV = \$63,492.06$
Therefore the NPV for Project A=
$\$38,095.23 + \$63,492.06 - \$100,000 = +\$1,587.29$

Project B
The Present Value of $42,000 received at the end of year 2:
$PV = FV/(1+i)^t$
$PV = \$42,000/(1.05)^2$
$PV = \$38.095.23$
The Present Value of $70,000 received at the end of year 3:
$PV = FV/(1+i)^t$
$PV = \$70,000/(1.05)^3$
$PV = \$60,468.61$
Therefore the NPV for Project B=
$\$38,095.23 + \$60,468.61 - \$100,000 = -\$1,436.16$

Bonus Question 6.
This bonus question comes from:

How to get every Statistical based Question right on the PMP®
Exam – PMP Exam Prep Simplified Series of mini-e-books
(50+ PMP® Exam Prep Sample Questions and Solutions
on standard deviation, variance, probability, Etc.)
(AME Group Coming late 2014)

You are the project manager for a logging company. This month you are charted to deliver 10,000 units that are 60 centimeters each. Your upper control limit on your process is 63 centimeters. Your lower control limit on your process is 57 centimeters. Approximately what percentage of your units will be above 61 centimeters?

a. 68.3%
b. 31.7%
c. 95.5%
d. 15.9%

Solution
Answer (d) is the beast answer.
15.9 % of the data will be above 61 centimeters.
Here are a few abbreviations we will use.
SD= one standard deviation
UCL = upper control limit
LCL = lower control limit
Also to solve this problem you need the equation for one standard deviation.
SD = | (UCL-LCL)/6 |
+/- 1 SD represents 68.23% of the data
+/- 2 SD represents 95.46% of the data
+/- 3 SD represents 99. 73% of the data

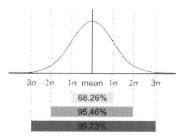

Q- what is one standard deviation?
SD = | (UCL-LCL)/6 |
SD = | (63-57)/6 |= | 6/6 |= 1 centimeter.
Q. What is the mean?
The mean is 60 centimeters.

Q. How many standard deviations is 61 centimeters from the mean?
61 centimeters is +1 standard deviation from the mean.
59 centimeters is -1 standard deviation from the mean.

Q. What percentage of the data falls between 59 and 61 centimeters?
Therefore, 68.3 % of the data will be between 59 and 61 centimeters.

Q. What percentage of the data falls outside of 59 through 61 centimeters?
If 68.3% of the data falls inside of this range than 100% - 68.3% must fall outside of the range.
100% - 68.3% = 31.7%. 31.7% will be outside of 59 centimeters and 61 centimeters.
Q. What percentage of the data falls above 61 centimeters?
Half of 31.7% will be above 61 centimeters and half of 31.7% will be below 59 centimeters.
 31.7/2= 15.9% will be above 61 centimeters.
Of course 31.7/2= 15.9% will be below 59 centimeters.

© AME Group Inc. August 2014

Bonus Question #7

A Fixed Price Incentive Fee (FPIF) contract has the following parameters:
Target Cost = $200,000
Target Profit = $20,000
Target Price = $220,000
Ceiling Price = $250,000
Share Ratio 70/30

The project was completed for an actual cost of $170,000. What is the actual profit the seller receives?

a. $9,000
b. $11,000
c. $20,000
d. $29,000

Solution:
Answer (d) is the best answer.
I solve FPIF problems that ask about actual profit and/or actual price by asking and answering a set of questions:
Q. What is the contract type?
A. FPIF

Q. Do we have an over run or under run and by how much?
A. The target cost is $200,000. Make sure you always look at target cost and not target price.
The actual cost is $170,000.

There is an under run of $30,000.

Q. Will the profit be adjusted up or down and by how much?
A. Since there is an under run the seller's profit will be adjusted up by the seller's percentage of the under run. The seller's percentage is 30%.
The seller's percentage is always the second number of the share ratio.
The adjustment to the seller's profit will be 30% of $30,000.
Profit adjustment = 30% * $30,000 = $9,000.

Q. What is the actual profit?
A. Actual profit = target profit + profit adjustment.
The $9,000 is being added since there is an under run.
The seller is being rewarded for the under run.
Actual profit = $20,000 + $9,000
Actual profit = $29,000
Since there is an under run we do not need to check the actual price against the ceiling price. With an under run the actual price could never

Thank you for reading!

Dear Reader,

I hope you enjoyed my first mini e-book: *How to get every Earned Value Question right on the exam.* I really enjoy helping people prepare for the PMP® Exam and Earned Value Management (EVM) is one of my favorite topics. Most importantly I hope the book is useful to you both for the PMP® Exam and for your project management career.

I wanted to request a small favor. If you were so inclined I'd love a review of *How to get every Earned Value Question right on the exam* on Amazon. Loved it , hated it (I hope not) - I would just enjoy to hear your feedback.

As you may have seen with Amazon, reviews can be tough to come by these days. You the reader have the power now to make or break a book. If you have time I would love you to go back to Amazon and write a quick review of the book. Thank you so much for reading for my first mini book: *How to get every Earned Value Question right on the exam.*

To write a review just go back to amazon and my book and click on reviews. Let me know if you would like to see more of these mini e-books. Specifically tell me the topics you would like covered and the language (English, Spanish, Portuguese, etc.) you will be using for your test.

Also to see all of my books please visit my <u>author page on Amazon.</u>
Regards,

Aileen

42863964R00084

Made in the USA
Middletown, DE
23 April 2017